States
PUERTO RICO

by Tyler Maine

CAPSTONE PRESS
a capstone imprint

Next Page Books are published by Capstone Press,
1710 Roe Crest Drive, North Mankato, Minnesota 56003
www.mycapstone.com

Library of Congress Cataloging-in-Publication Data
Cataloging-in-publication information is on file with the Library of
Congress.
ISBN 978-1-5157-0426-3 (library binding)
ISBN 978-1-5157-0485-0 (paperback)
ISBN 978-1-5157-0537-6 (ebook PDF)

Editorial Credits
Jaclyn Jaycox, editor; Kazuko Collins and Katy LaVigne, designers;
Morgan Walters, media researcher; Tori Abraham, production specialist

Photo Credits
Capstone Press: Angi Gahler, map 4, 7; Corbis: Bettmann, top 18;
Dreamstime: Amadeustx, 7, Joan Egert, top 21; Getty Images: Getty
Images Sport/Clive Brunskill, top 19; Newscom: Angel M. Rivera /
STAFF/El Nuevo Dia de Puerto Rico, 29, Everett Collection, 28, Icon
SMI/John Cordes, middle 19, Splash News/Photopress PR, bottom
18; North Wind Picture Archives, 12, 27; One Mile Up, Inc., flag,
seal 23; Shutterstock: a katz, 17, Colin D. Young, cover, eddtoro,
10, Everett Historical, 25, Featureflash, middle 18, IrinaK, bottom
21, jiawangkun, 13, Jiri Vatka, 11, LivetImages, bottom right 8,
magnetix, top 24, panda3800, bottom 24, Paul Dempsey, bottom left 8,
PhotographyByMK, 14, pyzata, 9, s_bukley, bottom 19, sakhorn, top 20,
Sean Pavone, 5, Songquan Deng, 16, Subbotina Anna, bottom 20, Valery
Bareta, 6, 15, Zadorozhna Natalia, 26

All design elements by Shutterstock

Printed and bound in China.
0316/CA21600187
012016 009436F16

TABLE OF CONTENTS

Want to take your research further? Ask your librarian if your school subscribes to PebbleGo Next. If so, when you see this helpful symbol (►) throughout the book, log onto www.pebblegonext.com for bonus downloads and information.

LOCATION

Puerto Rico is a semitropical island in the Caribbean Sea. It lies about 1,000 miles (1,600 kilometers) southeast of Florida. It's part of an island chain called the Greater Antilles. Puerto Rico is made up of a large main island and several smaller islands. Puerto Rico is smaller than 48 of the 50 states. The Atlantic Ocean lies north of Puerto Rico, and the Caribbean Sea lies to the south. The capital and largest city in Puerto Rico is San Juan. Bayamón and Carolina are Puerto Rico's next largest cities.

**PebbleGo Next Bonus!
To print and label your own map, go to www.pebblegonext.com and search keywords:**

PR MAP

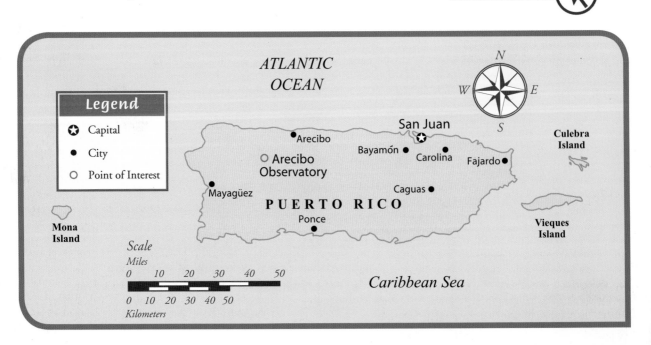

San Juan is located on a small island connected to Puerto Rico's mainland by three bridges.

GEOGRAPHY

Sandy beaches line the northern and southern Coastal Lowlands along the outside of the island. The Coastal Valley regions on the east and west coasts extend inland into Puerto Rico's foothills and mountains. The foothills rise on the eastern and western sides of the island. They extend into Puerto Rico's mountains in the center of the island. The main mountain range is the Cordillera Central. It runs east and west through the middle of the island. Puerto Rico's highest peak is Cerro de Punta. It rises 4,389 feet (1,338 meters) in the Cordillera Central.

To watch a video about the Arecibo telescope, go to www.pebblegonext.com and search keywords:

PR VIDEO

Puerto Rico's beaches draw millions of tourists each year.

The whole island of Puerto Rico can be seen from the summit of Cerro de Punta, including San Juan, which is 75 miles (121 km) away.

ATLANTIC
OCEAN

COASTAL LOWLANDS
Grande de Arecibo
Grande de Loíza
Culebra Island
COASTAL VALLEYS
FOOTHILLS
Cerro de Punta
Río de la Plata
CENTRAL MOUNTAINS
FOOTHILLS
COSTAL VALLEYS
CORDILLERA CENTRAL
COASTAL LOWLANDS

Mona Island

Vieques Island

Caribbean Sea

Scale
Miles
0   10   20   30   40   50

0 10 20 30 40 50
Kilometers

N
W   E
S

Legend

Caribbean National Forest

▲ Highest Point

Mountain Range

River

WEATHER

Puerto Rico's tropical climate is steady throughout the year. The temperature averages between 73 and 80 degrees Fahrenheit (23 and 27 degrees Celsius). Sea breezes make the warm temperatures more comfortable.

Average High and Low Temperatures (San Juan, PR)

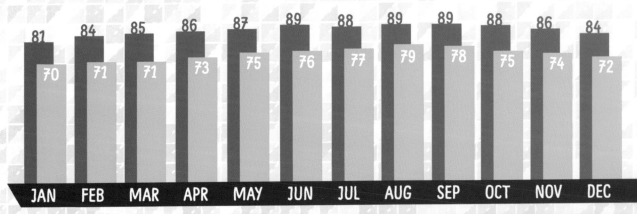

	JAN	FEB	MAR	APR	MAY	JUN	JUL	AUG	SEP	OCT	NOV	DEC
High	81	84	85	86	87	89	88	89	89	88	86	84
Low	70	71	71	73	75	76	77	79	78	75	74	72

LANDMARKS

El Yunque

Caribbean National Forest, also known as El Yunque, is the United States' only tropical rain forest. El Yunque has been set aside for people to enjoy. The El Portal Visitors Center teaches people about the rain forest.

San Juan National Historic Site

In the 1600s San Juan and San Juan Bay were protected from intruders by a series of forts and walls. This historic site preserves these forts and walls. More than 2 million people visit the site every year.

Arecibo Observatory

In the mountains of western Puerto Rico is the Arecibo Observatory, one of the world's most important space research centers. Arecibo's telescope is the largest single-dish radio telescope in the world.

HISTORY AND GOVERNMENT

Juan Ponce de León officially became the first governor of Puerto Rico in 1509.

By AD 1000 Taíno Indians had settled in present-day Puerto Rico. In 1493 Christopher Columbus landed on Puerto Rico but did not stay. In 1508 Spanish explorer Juan Ponce de Leon established the first Spanish settlement. San Juan became an important port for Spain. Strong forts were built to protect the island. In 1897 Puerto Rico gained many self-governing powers. In 1898 U.S. forces invaded Puerto Rico as part of the Spanish-American War. When Spain lost, it gave Puerto Rico to the United States. It became a commonwealth in 1952. It's like a state but Puerto Ricans do not pay taxes to the U.S. government.

Puerto Rico's legislative branch of government makes the commonwealth's laws. It consists of a 27-member Senate and a 51-member House of Representatives. Puerto Rico's governor is the head of the executive branch. Judges and their courts make up the judicial branch. They uphold the laws.

Although Puerto Rico residents are U.S. citizens, they cannot vote in U.S. presidential elections.

INDUSTRY

Manufacturing is the island's largest industry. Puerto Rico's main manufactured products are medicine, chemicals, clothing, electronics, and food products. Puerto Rico has four sugar mills that produce raw sugar from sugarcane, which is grown in the Coastal Lowlands. The flavoring ingredients for Coca-Cola and Pepsi are made in the town of Cidra.

Tourism is an important source of income for the island. Puerto Rico's tropical climate and beautiful beaches attract nearly 4 million tourists each year.

Puerto Rico's main crop is coffee. Coffee beans are grown in the Central Mountains.

Puerto Rico is the leading coffee producer for the United States.

Puerto Rico's tourism industry contributes more than $7 billion to the economy each year.

POPULATION

Puerto Rico is home to about 3.6 million people. The island is more crowded than any U.S. state. Most Puerto Ricans live in or near large cities.

Most Puerto Ricans have diverse backgrounds. Almost all Puerto Ricans trace their history back to the Spanish colonists. These colonists intermarried with Taíno Indians and African slaves. Other ethnic groups, such as Haitians, Europeans, and Cubans, came to Puerto Rico. All these races and cultures mixed. This new unique race and culture can only be described as Puerto Rican. Despite their

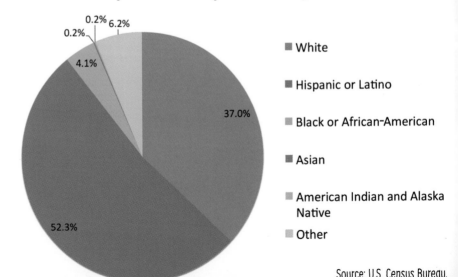

Population by Ethnicity

- 0.2%
- 0.2%
- 6.2%
- 4.1%
- 37.0%
- 52.3%

- ■ White
- ■ Hispanic or Latino
- ■ Black or African-American
- ■ Asian
- ■ American Indian and Alaska Native
- ■ Other

Source: U.S. Census Bureau.

varied backgrounds, most Puerto Ricans consider themselves Hispanic. Puerto Ricans do not separate themselves by ethnic or cultural backgrounds.

FAMOUS PEOPLE

Roberto Clemente (1934–1972) was one of baseball's greatest outfielders, as well as a great hitter. He played for the Pittsburgh Pirates. He was born in Carolina. He died in a plane crash while trying to help earthquake victims in Nicaragua.

Ricky Martin (1971–) is a popular singer. His first big hit was "Livin' la Vida Loca" (1999). He was born Enrique José Martin Morales IV in San Juan.

Juan "Chi-chi" Rodríguez (1937–) was born in Río Piedras. He was the first Puerto Rican to be inducted into the World Golf Hall of Fame.

Gigi Fernández (1964–) is a former pro tennis player. She was the first Puerto Rican woman to turn professional and the first ever to win an Olympic gold medal. She was also the first Puerto Rican woman to be inducted into the International Tennis Hall of Fame. She was born in San Juan.

Carlos Beltrán (1977–) plays baseball for the New York Yankees. He was born in Manati.

José Feliciano (1945–) is a singer and guitarist who has won many Grammy awards. "Light My Fire" is one of his best-known songs. He also wrote the Christmas song "Feliz Navidad." He was born in Lares.

COMMONWEALTH SYMBOLS

Tree

silk-cotton tree

Flower

Puerto Rican hibiscus

Bird

stripe-headed tanager

Animal

coquí

PebbleGo Next Bonus! To make a dessert using an ingredient grown in Puerto Rico, go to www.pebblegonext.com and search keywords:

PR RECIPE

FAST FACTS

DATE OF U.S. COMMONWEALTH
1952

CAPITAL ☆
San Juan

LARGEST CITY ●
San Juan

SIZE
3,424 square miles (8,868 square kilometers) land area (2010 U.S. Census Bureau)

POPULATION
3,615,086 (2013 U.S. Census estimate)

COMMONWEALTH NICKNAME
Island of Enchantment

COMMONWEALTH MOTTO
"Joannes est nomen ejus," which is Latin for "Juan is his name"

COMMONWEALTH SEAL

The seal of the Commonwealth of Puerto Rico dates back to the 1500s. In the green center, the lamb represents peace. The two letters F and I stand for the Spanish rulers, Ferdinand and Isabella, at the time of the island's discovery. The sentence below in Latin, "Johannes est nomen ejus" means "Juan is his name." The towers of Castile, the lions of Leon, the crosses of Jerusalem, and Spanish flags lie around the green circle. These symbols show Puerto Rico's Hispanic heritage.

PebbleGo Next Bonus!
To print and color
your own flag, go to
www.pebblegonext.com
and search keywords:

PR FLAG

COMMONWEALTH FLAG

The Puerto Rican flag was designed in New York by people who were fighting for the island's independence. The flag was first used on December 22, 1895. The flag was officially adopted when Puerto Rico became a commonwealth on July 25, 1952. Five alternate red and white stripes meet a triangle on the left. The triangle holds a single white star inside it. The white star stands for the Commonwealth of Puerto Rico.

MINING PRODUCTS

portland cement and stone, clay, lime, salt

MANUFACTURED GOODS

medicine, chemicals, machinery, electronics

FARM PRODUCTS

coffee, sugarcane, bananas, pineapples, avocados, coconuts

PebbleGo Next Bonus!
To learn the lyrics to
the state song, go to
www.pebblegonext.com
and search keywords:

PR SONG

PUERTO RICO TIMELINE

CIRCA 1000

Taíno Indians from South America settle on the island; they call the island Boriken or Borinquen, which means "land of the great lords."

1493

Christopher Columbus claims present-day Puerto Rico for Spain and names the island San Juan Bautista.

1508

Spanish explorer Juan Ponce de Leon founds the island's first European settlement.

1620

The Pilgrims establish a colony in the New World in present-day Massachusetts.

1678 Five miles (8 km) of stone walls are built around San Juan to help keep the city safe from intruders.

1700s Coffee becomes an important export product for Puerto Rico.

1861–1865 The Union and the Confederacy fight the Civil War.

1868 Puerto Ricans in Lares rebel against Spanish rule; Spanish soldiers put down the revolt.

1897 Spain allows Puerto Rico to govern itself.

1898 The United States gains control of Puerto Rico.

1914–1918 World War I is fought; the United States enters the war in 1917.

1917 The U.S. Congress makes Puerto Ricans U.S. citizens.

1939–1945

World War II is fought; the United States enters the war in 1941.

1947

The U.S. Congress allows Puerto Ricans to elect their own governor.

1952

On July 25 Puerto Rico becomes a U.S. commonwealth.

1983

San Juan's fort system becomes a World Heritage Site. Sites on this list have cultural or natural importance to the world.

1998

On September 21 Hurricane Georges strikes Puerto Rico, killing three people and causing more than $2 billion in damage.

2000

Puerto Rico's first female governor, Sila Calderón, takes office.

2011

President Barack Obama becomes the first president since John F. Kennedy to make an official visit to Puerto Rico.

2015

Puerto Rico suffers a record-breaking heat wave and severe drought.

Glossary

commonwealth *(KOM-uhn-welth)*—a nation or state that is governed by the people who live there

diversity *(di-VUR-suh-tee)*—the condition of being varied

ethnic *(ETH-nik)*—related to a group of people and their culture

executive *(ig-ZE-kyuh-tiv)*—the branch of government that makes sure laws are followed

export *(EK-sport)*—to send products to another country to be sold there

industry *(IN-duh-stree)*—a business which produces a product or provides a service

intrude *(in-trood)*—to force your way into a place or situation where you are not wanted or invited

legislature *(LEJ-iss-lay-chur)*—a group of elected officials who have the power to make or change laws for a country or state

region *(REE-juhn)*—a large area

tourism *(TOOR-i-zuhm)*—the business of taking care of visitors to a country or place

tropical *(TROP-uh-kuhl)*—to do with or living in the hot, rainy area of the tropics

Read More

Bjorklund, Ruth. *Puerto Rico: The Island of Enchantment*. It's My State! New York: Cavendish Square Publishing, 2016.

Ganeri, Anita. *United States of America: A Benjamin Blog and His Inquisitive Dog Guide*. Country Guides. Chicago: Heinemann Raintree, 2015.

Yasuda, Anita. *What's Great About Puerto Rico?* Our Great States. Minneapolis: Lerner Publications Company, 2015.

Internet Sites

FactHound offers a safe, fun way to find Internet sites related to this book. All of the sites on FactHound have been researched by our staff.

Here's all you do:

Visit *www.facthound.com*

Type in this code: 9781515704263

 Check out projects, games and lots more at **www.capstonekids.com**

Critical Thinking Using the Common Core

1. Puerto Rico is smaller than how many of the 50 states? (Key Ideas and Details)

2. Most Puerto Ricans have diverse backgrounds. What does diversity mean? (Craft and Structure)

3. Look at the pie chart on page 16. What percentage of Puerto Rico's population is Hispanic or Latino? (Craft and Structure)

Index

972.95 M
Maine, Tyler,
Puerto Rico /

FLT

04/17